# A Huntingdon Celebration

## Philip Sparke

*for Concert Band*

Edition number: AMP 043

**Philip Sparke**
**A HUNTINGDON CELEBRATION**

© 2003 by **Anglo Music Press**,
PO Box 303, Wembley, HA9 8GX, England
*Copyright secured / All rights reserved*

Recording on: **CD** *KALEIDOSCOPE*
The J.W.F. Military Band
CD number: AR 007-3

**Philip Sparke**

Philip Sparke was born in London in 1951 and studied composition, trumpet and piano at the Royal College of Music, where he gained an ARCM. It was at the College that his interest in bands arose. He played in the college wind band and formed a brass band among the students, writing several works for both ensembles. At that time, Sparke's first published works appeared – *Concert Prelude* (brass band) and *Gaudium* (wind band). A growing interest in his music led to several commissions, his first major one being for the Centennial Brass Band Championships in New Zealand – *The Land of the Long White Cloud*. Further commissions followed from individual bands, various band associations and the BBC, for whom he three times won the EBU New Music for Band Competition (with *Slipstream, Skyrider* and *Orient Express*). Sparke has written for brass band championships in New Zealand, Switzerland, The Netherlands, Australia and the UK, twice for the National Finals at the Albert Hall, and his test pieces are constantly in use wherever brass bands can be found. A close association with banding in Japan led to a commission (*Celebration*) from and eventual recording of his music with the Tokyo Kosei Wind Orchestra. This opened the door world-wide to his wind band music and led to several commissions, particularly from the United States. In 1996, the US Air Force Band commissioned and recorded *Dance Movements*, which won the prestigious Sudler Prize in 1997. Philip Sparke's conducting and adjudicating activities have taken him to most European countries, Australia, New Zealand, Japan and the USA.

Philip Sparke wurde 1951 in London geboren. Er studierte Komposition, Trompete und Klavier am Royal College of Music und wurde dort als ARCM (Associate of the Royal College of Music) ausgezeichnet. Sein Interesse an Musik für Bandformationen geht auf diese Zeit zurück. Er spielte im Blasorchester des Colleges, gründete mit anderen Studenten eine Brass Band und schrieb für beide Ensembles etliche Stücke. Gleichzeitig wurden mit *Concert Prelude* für Brass Band und *Gaudium* für Blasorchester erste Arbeiten von ihm veröffentlicht. Seine Stücke erregten zunehmend Aufmerksamkeit und dies hatte eine Reihe von Auftragskompositionen zur Folge. *The Land of the Long White Cloud* für die Centennial Brass Band Championships in Neuseeland war darunter das erste größere Werk. Es folgten weitere Auftragskompositionen für verschiedene Bands, diverse Band-Zusammenschlüsse und die BBC, für die er mit *Slipstream, Skyrider* und *Orient Express* dreimal den EBU New Music for Band Competition gewann. Er hat für Brass Band-Wettbewerbe in Neuseeland, der Schweiz, Holland, Australien und Großbritannien komponiert, zweimal auch für die landesweite Endausscheidung in der Albert Hall. Seine Teststücke sind weltweit aus dem Brass Band-Bereich nicht wegzudenken.

Die enge Zusammenarbeit mit Bands in Japan brachte ihm mit *Celebration* einen weiteren Kompositionsauftrag ein und führte zur Einspielung seiner Musik durch das Kosei Wind Orchestra Tokyo. Dadurch öffneten sich seiner Musik weltweit Türen und Tore und er erhielt weitere Aufträge, vor allem aus den USA. 1996 wurde *Dance Movements* von der US Airforce Band bestellt und aufgenommen. Das Werk gewann 1997 den begehrten Sudler Prize. Seine Tätigkeit als Dirigent und Ratgeber haben ihn in die meisten europäischen Länder, nach Australien, Neuseeland, Japan und die Vereinigten Staaten geführt.

Né en 1951 à Londres, Philip Sparke étudie la composition, la trompette et le piano au célèbre Royal College of Music de Londres où il obtient l'Associate Diploma (ARCM). Durant ses études, il commence à s'intéresser aux formations d'instruments à vent. Il joue dans l'Orchestre d'Harmonie du Collège de Musique, forme un Brass Band avec d'autres étudiants et compose plusieurs pièces dont deux seront publiées : *Concert Prelude* pour Brass Band et *Gaudium*, une œuvre pour Orchestre d'Harmonie. Sa musique suscite un intérêt grandissant et plusieurs commandes lui parviennent. La première commande importante qu'il reçoit est celle d'une œuvre pour un concours de Brass Bands en Nouvelle-Zélande – les Centennial Brass Band Championships. Il compose pour cette occasion *The Land of the Long White Cloud*. D'autres commandes suivent ; elles lui sont adressées par des Orchestres à Vent, par différentes fédérations d'orchestres et par la BBC, pour laquelle il remportera trois fois le concours pour Orchestres d'Harmonie de l'Union Européenne de Radio-Télévision (avec les pièces *Slipstream*, *Skyrider* et *Orient Express*). Aujourd'hui, les compositions de Philip Sparke figurent régulièrement au programme des concours de Brass Bands du monde entier (Nouvelle-Zélande, Australie, Pays-Bas, Suisse, Grande-Bretagne,…). Très présent dans le domaine de la musique pour Orchestre d'Harmonie au Japon, Philip Sparke compose une œuvre de commande (*Celebration*) pour l'Orchestre d'Harmonie Tokyo Kosei qui enregistrera par la suite plusieurs de ses compositions contribuant ainsi à la diffusion à l'échelle mondiale de sa musique pour Orchestre d'Harmonie. De nombreuses autres commandes lui parviendront alors, notamment des États-Unis. En 1996, il écrit *Dance Movements*, une œuvre de commande pour la Musique de l'US Air Force, qui sera récompensée du prestigieux Prix International de Composition Sudler en 1997. Parallèlement à sa carrière de compositeur, ses activités de chef d'orchestre et de membre de jury le conduisent à se rendre dans la plupart des pays d'Europe, en Australie, en Nouvelle-Zélande, au Japon et aux États-Unis.

Philip Sparke werd in 1951 in Londen geboren en studeerde compositie, trompet en piano aan het Royal College of Music. Tijdens deze opleiding groeide zijn belangstelling voor blaasorkesten. Hij speelde in het harmonieorkest van het college, vormde een brassband met medestudenten en schreef verschillende werken voor beide orkesten. In deze tijd werden zijn eerste werken gepubliceerd: *Concert Prelude* (voor brassband) en *Gaudium* (voor harmonieorkest). Een groeiende belangstelling voor zijn muziek resulteerde in verschillende opdrachten. Zijn eerste grote werk schreef hij voor de Centennial Brass Band Championships in Nieuw-Zeeland en was getiteld *The Land of the Long White Cloud*. Meer opdrachten volgden van orkesten, verschillende orkestorganisaties en de BBC, waarmee hij driemaal de EBU New Music for Band Competition won (met *Slipstream, Skyrider* en *Orient Express*). Hij componeerde voor de brassbandkampioenschappen van Nieuw-Zeeland, Zwitserland, Nederland, Australië en Groot-Brittannië en tweemaal voor de Britse National Finals in de Royal Albert Hall. Overal waar brassbands zijn, worden zijn werken gespeeld. Goede betrekkingen met orkesten in Japan leidden uiteindelijk tot een opdracht (*Celebration*) van het Tokyo Kosei Wind Orchestra, dat ook zijn muziek opnam. Dit resulteerde in een wereldwijde belangstelling voor zijn muziek voor harmonieorkest, wat leidde tot verschillende opdrachten, voornamelijk vanuit de Verenigde Staten. In 1996 nam de US Air Force Band de door hun verstrekte compositieopdracht *Dance Movements* op. Met dit werk won Philip Sparke in 1997 de prestigieuze Sudler Prize. Sparkes dirigeer- en juryactiviteiten brachten hem naar de meeste Europese landen, Australië, Nieuw-Zeeland, Japan en de Verenigde Staten.

# A Huntingdon Celebration

The Huntingdonshire Concert Band, based in the east of England, is a community band, which was founded in 1993. In 2001, they invited composer Philip Sparke to work with them on some of his pieces for a weekend. This led to the band asking Sparke to write a piece to celebrate their 10th Anniversary in 2003. *A Huntingdon Celebration* was the result.

This short and lively overture opens with a fanfare-like passage based on the main theme, which soon appears on clarinets and saxophones and is then taken up by the whole band. Answering phrases between brass and woodwind lead to a second *legato* theme over bubbling eighth notes. This in turn leads to a slower central chorale in the tenor register of the band. The original tempo returns and, after a period of thematic development, the main theme reappears until the opening fanfare returns to bring the piece to a close.

Die Huntingdonshire Concert Band, mit Sitz im Osten Englands, ist ein kommunales Blasorchester, das 1993 gegründet wurde. Im Jahr 2001 wurde der Komponist Philip Sparke eingeladen, um mit ihnen ein Wochenende lang an einigen seiner Stücke zu arbeiten. Dies führte dazu, dass man Sparke bat, ein Stück zur Feier des zehnjährigen Bestehens des Blasorchesters 2003 zu schreiben. Das Ergebnis war *A Huntingdon Celebration*.

Diese kurze, lebhafte Ouvertüre beginnt mit einer fanfareähnlichen Passage, die auf dem Hauptthema basiert, welches alsbald in den Klarinetten und Saxophonen erscheint und dann vom gesamten Blasorchester aufgenommen wird. Sich beantwortende Phrasen zwischen dem Blech- und dem Holzbläserregister führen zu einem zweiten, gebundenen Thema über perlenden Achtelnoten. Dies führt wiederum zu einem langsameren zentralen Choral im Tenorregister des Blasorchesters. Das ursprüngliche Tempo kehrt zurück und, nach einer Phase der thematischen Entwicklung, erscheint wieder das Hauptthema, bis die Eröffnungsfanfare zurückkehrt, um das Stück zu beenden.

L'Orchestre d'Harmonie du Comté du Huntingdonshire, situé dans l'Est de l'Angleterre, a été fondé en 1993. En 2001, les musiciens invitent le compositeur Philip Sparke, pour un week-end de travail consacré à ses œuvres. De cette collaboration chaleureuse, naît l'idée de passer commande d'une pièce pour le 10ème anniversaire de la création de la formation, célébré en 2003. Philip Sparke leur compose *A Huntingdon Celebration*.

Cette ouverture courte et vive débute avec une introduction écrite en forme de fanfare qui s'inspire du thème principal, exposé, dans un premier temps, par les clarinettes et les saxophones, puis par l'Orchestre d'Harmonie en entier. Cuivres et bois établissent une conversation musicale qui mène à l'introduction d'un second thème tout en *legato*, sur un accompagnement bouillonnant en croches. Le passage central, plus lent, développe un choral dans les registres ténors. Le tempo premier revient ensuite et le thème initial est exposé à nouveau, amorçant la reprise de la fanfare d'ouverture qui vient conclure l'œuvre sur une note brillante.

De Huntingdonshire Concert Band, uit het oosten van Engeland, is een gemeentelijk blaasorkest dat is opgericht in 1993. In 2001 werd de componist Philip Sparke gevraagd om met het orkest een weekend lang aan een aantal stukken te werken. Naar aanleiding hiervan kreeg hij het verzoek een stuk te schrijven ter gelegenheid van het tienjarig bestaan in 2003. Het resultaat was *A Huntingdon Celebration*.

Deze korte en levendige ouverture begint met een fanfareachtige passage die is gebaseerd op het hoofdthema, dat al snel verschijnt in de klarinetten en saxofoons, waarna het hele orkest het oppikt. Vraag-en-antwoordfrasen tussen het koper en het hout leiden naar een tweede *legato* thema over parelende achtste noten. Dit thema leidt weer naar een langzamer centraal koraal in het tenorregister van het orkest. Het oorspronkelijke tempo keert terug en na een thematische ontwikkeling komt het hoofdthema weer naar voren totdat de openingsfanfare terugkeert en het stuk besluit.

## Concert Band

| | |
|---|---|
| Full Score | 1 |
| Piccolo | 1 |
| Flute 1 | 2 |
| Flute 2 | 2 |
| Oboe | 2 |
| E♭ Clarinet | 1 |
| B♭ Clarinet 1 | 5 |
| B♭ Clarinet 2 | 5 |
| B♭ Clarinet 3 | 5 |
| E♭ Alto Clarinet | 1 |
| B♭ Bass Clarinet | 1 |
| Bassoon | 2 |
| E♭ Alto Saxophone 1 | 1 |
| E♭ Alto Saxophone 2 | 1 |
| B♭ Tenor Saxophone | 2 |
| E♭ Baritone Saxophone | 1 |
| B♭ Trumpet 1 | 2 |
| B♭ Trumpet 2 | 2 |
| B♭ Trumpet 3 | 2 |
| F Horn 1 | 1 |
| F Horn 2 | 1 |
| F Horn 3 | 1 |
| F Horn 4 | 1 |
| Trombone 1 | 2 |
| Trombone 2 | 2 |
| Trombone 3 | 2 |
| Euphonium | 2 |
| B♭ Euphonium T.C. | 2 |
| Tuba | 4 |
| Double Bass | 1 |
| Timpani | 1 |
| Percussion 1 | 1 |
| Percussion 2 | 1 |
| Percussion 3 | 1 |

## Supplementary Parts

| | |
|---|---|
| E♭ Horn 1 | 1 |
| E♭ Horn 2 | 1 |
| E♭ Horn 3 | 1 |
| E♭ Horn 4 | 1 |
| B♭ Trombone 1 T.C. and B.C. | 1 |
| B♭ Trombone 2 T.C. and B.C. | 1 |
| B♭ Trombone 3 T.C. and B.C. | 1 |
| B♭ Euphonium T.C. | 2 |
| B♭ Euphonium B.C. | 2 |
| E♭ Tuba T.C. and B.C. | 2 |
| B♭ Tuba T.C. and B.C. | 2 |

# A Huntingdon Celebration
## Philip Sparke

Recording on: **CD** *KALEIDOSCOPE*
The Johan Willem Friso Military Band
CD number: AR 007-3

Commissioned by the Huntingdonshire Concert Band to celebrate their 10th Anniversary

# A HUNTINGDON CELEBRATION

Philip Sparke

Recorded on:
KALEIDOSCOPE
AR 007-3

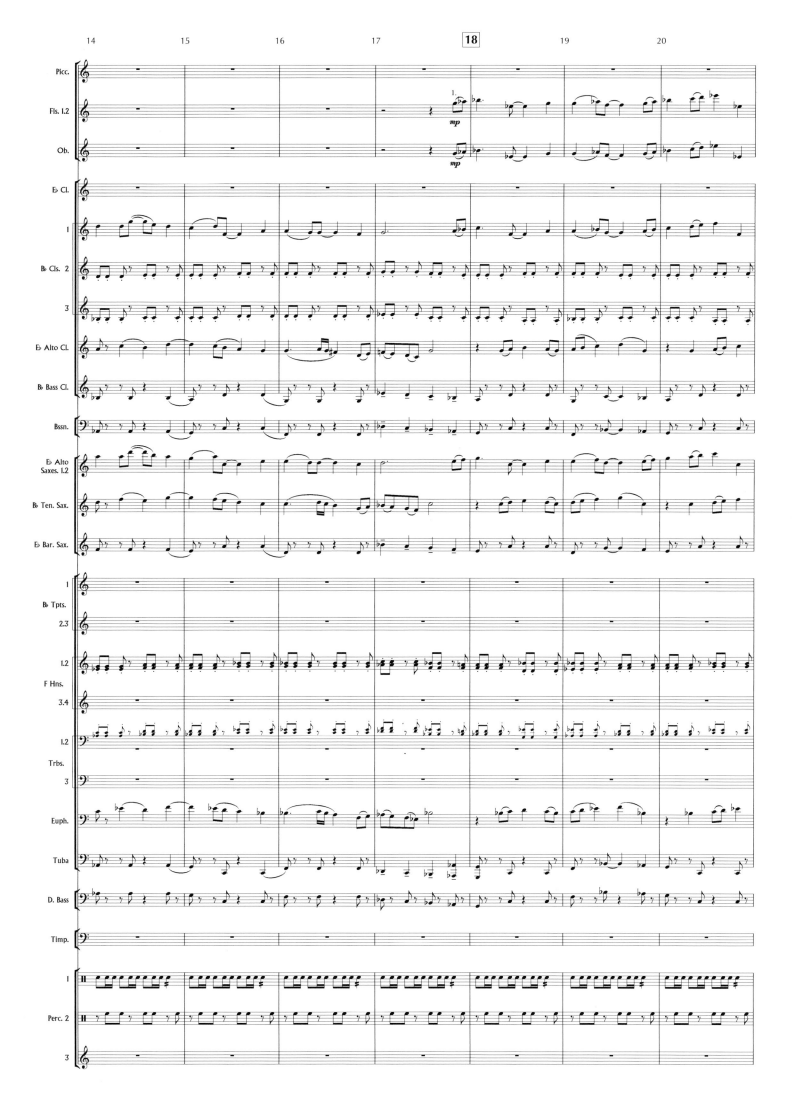

9

13

15

16

26

28

29